ARE WE THERE YET?
ALL ABOUT THE PLANET JUPITER!
SPACE FOR KIDS
Children's Aeronautics & Space Book

BABY PROFESSOR

EDUCATION KIDS

Speedy Publishing LLC
40 E. Main St. #1156
Newark, DE 19711
www.speedypublishing.com

Jupiter is the fifth planet from the Sun.

Jupiter is
the largest
planet in the
solar system.

Jupiter is so big that all the other planets in the solar system would fit inside it.

Jupiter is a gas giant because it doesn't have a solid surface.

Jupiter has
62 identified
moons.

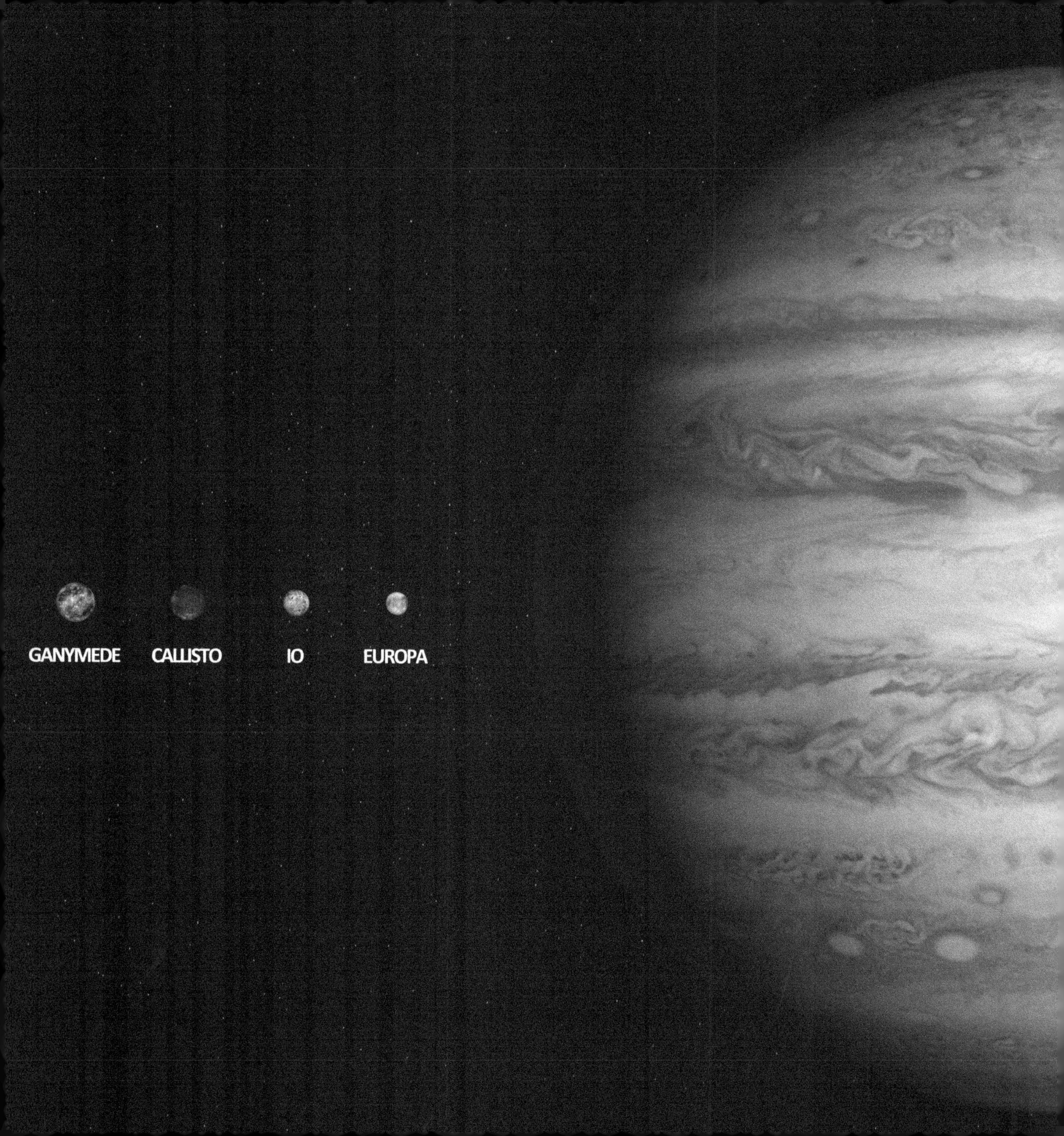
GANYMEDE
CALLISTO
IO
EUROPA

The largest moon is Ganymede, it is larger than Mercury and Pluto.

When Jupiter and Earth are closest to each other they are approximately 391 million miles apart.

EARTH

JUPITER

The centre of Jupiter is a rocky core and is slightly bigger than Earth.

Jupiter is a stormy planet. The most notable is the big red spot which is the largest hurricane in our Solar System.

The red spot is also called "The Eye of Jupiter" because of its shape.

The distance between Jupiter and the Sun is approximately 466 million miles.

Jupiter has a diameter of 88,701 miles.

Jupiter spins on its axis once every 9.84 hours. It is the fastest spinning planet in the Solar System.

The first person to discover Jupiter's moons was Galileo Galilei.

Jupiter's temperature is -170 degrees Fahrenheit.

If you weigh 220 pounds on Earth, on Jupiter you would weigh 330 pounds.

Jupiter also has rings similar to that of Saturn but are much less visible.

JUPITER

JUPITER

There are three rings in all and are named Gossamer, Halo and Main.

Surrounding Jupiter's core is a sea of liquid hydrogen.

Our planets are unique in their own special way.

Visit

BABY PROFESSOR
EDUCATION KIDS

www.BabyProfessorBooks.com

to download Free Baby Professor eBooks
and view our catalog of new and exciting
Children's Books

CPSIA information can be obtained
at www.ICGtesting.com
Printed in the USA
LVHW060515070119
602983LV00008B/321/P